Selfless Rose

Solo Poetry Collection

Dr. Archita Biswas

BookLeaf Publishing

India | USA | UK

Made with ❤ on the BookLeaf Publishing Platform
www.bookleafpub.in
www.bookleafpub.com

Dedication

I dedicate my first book of English poems, *Selfless Rose,* to my parents, Dr. Nirupama Saha and the late Dr. Ashoke Kumar Saha, who instilled in me the virtue of humility.

Acknowledgement

Firstly, I would like to express my heartfelt gratitude to my children, Shukttij and Neilaabjo, who are my life's fountain. I am grateful for their co-operation, patience, and the precious time that they have spared so that I could pursue my creativity.

I am thankful to my husband Surajit Biswas, for being my critic and offering support in my creative pursuits.

Lastly, my deepest appreciation goes to my mother, Dr. Nirupama Saha, whose unwavering support and encouragement have been the guiding force in all my endeavours. I can never thank her enough for her constant belief in me.

Preface

Dear Reader,

Selfless Rose is my first collection of English poems, born from my love for rhyming words and my desire to capture emotions in their purest form—brief yet profound. This book is my humble endeavour to share with you the thoughts and images that found their way onto these pages, just as they came to me.

Whether read in solitude or shared with loved ones, this book is for students, teachers, and all poetry enthusiasts. It serves as a valuable resource for elocution, offering poems that are deeply personal yet universally relatable—perfect for both quiet reflection and spoken performance.

With *Selfless Rose* I extend my best wishes to you. I sincerely thank you for joining me in my journey of poems.

With poetry and passion,
Archita Biswas.

CONTENTS

Selfless Rose

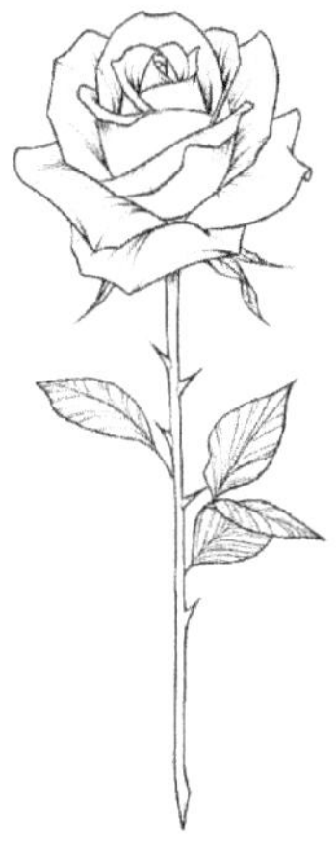

To the rose in my garden, I enquired:
"O crimson rose, tell me—why do you blush
When you look up at the sky above?
Why do you fill the air with fragrance?
Tell me, with whom have you fallen in love?
You look ever-so-bright and charming!
Tell me your secret my sweet darling."

In a shy little voice the rose replied:
"I'm in love with the wide world around-
And all that I have, I want to share.

I wish to bring joy to every heart,
So with my fragrance, I fill the air.
I want nothing more to brighten my day.
I'll love you all till I wither away."

Coming Of The Rains

In the sweltering heat of the summer day,
O, how I long for you!
To come and drench the thirsty earth,
And make it lively anew.

Then comes the rumbling of the clouds,
As drops fall on the terrain -
And comes the rapturous downpour.
Rain! O, beautiful rain!

The Balance Rope

Life is a tight balance rope,
And we - mere puppets in the hands of God.
Yet, in vacant space we grope,
Little remembering that He holds the cord.

To His tune, He makes us dance,
With unseen hands He pull our strings.
And when He wills, we lose balance,
And, the curtain down He brings.

Mind-bird

My mind is like a bird in flight,
Soaring high and high,
To reach a cherished dreamland—
A realm beyond the sky.

My mind soars with out-stretched wings,
Flapping in rhythm.
Their soft and bright feathers
Are my fancied dreams.

My mind-bird seeks to reach
To the land of rainbows,
Where assurance of peace and love
Like a river flows.

Darkness - A Passing Phase

When in darkness, do not fear,
Keep your candle burning bright.
Everything uncanny will disappear,
Just follow your candle light.

The darkness of the night,
Is but just a messenger
Who reminds us that the light
Of a new dawn is not very far.

Dark days are but a fleeting phase;
When they come we yearn for light -
A new light that exposes all fakes
And makes our vision all the more bright.

The Sky

When I gaze at the vast blue sky
And watch the white clouds drifting by,
Its endless expanse fills me with awe.

The magnanimous sky spreads arms invisible
To embrace me during times of trouble,
To provide solace like the dearest pal.

The softness of the sky nurtures my soul,
The vastness makes me one with the whole,
Like a flag of glory the sky spreads above me.

The endless sky forever assure
That I shall always be secure,
With the Eternal blue roof to shelter me.

Sweet Remembrance

Today,
As I walk down memory's lane,
The good old days
Come back to me once again.
Those golden moments I still cherish,
Some fulfilled dreams,
Or some unfulfilled wish.
When I close my eyes,,
I can see
The faces of my loved ones
Just before me.
On a silent afternoon,
I seem to hear
Their voices and laughter
Ring true and clear.
The old memories
Have a wondrous charm!

Even on gloomy days
They can keep me warm.
The air seems to carry
Some long lost fragrance.
Ah! The sweet remembrance.

I Want To Be

When I was a little child,
People often asked me,
"When you grow up, little one,
What do you wish to be?"
"A doctor or a scientist,
Something grand, you see—
Or perhaps a painter....,"
I'd answer timidly.
But to tell the truth-
I wasn't quite sure, exactly.

So, I strove to gain
The finest education,
So that I may fulfill
Some great ambition.
And tried to work hard
Towards some bright destination.
Sometimes I met with success,
And happiness knew no bounds.
Sometimes there were failures -
A part of life, I later found.

But
A lot of qualities one should have,
Not just glories to your name.
One doesn't achieve everything
If he only achieves fame.
To lose the humaneness we're born with
Is the deepest shame.
Now, I know my heart's desire,
But people won't understand, you see.
"A nice and true human being"-
That's what I always want to be.

Those Unspoken Words

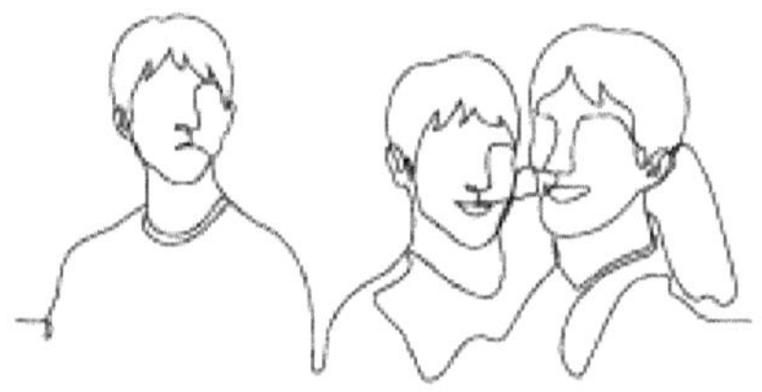

Those unspoken words, which lips never carved out,
Those very words - which other people talked about.
Words which took a deeper hue with every passing day,
Those words - which in vain my eyes tried to say.
Those unspoken words—which you could never understand,
Words that were mine, with me forever remained.
Those words, which were stifled deep inside my heart,
Till that day, when our own ways we did part.

I thought, those words had died a silent
death,
My unexpressed love - I garlanded with a
wreath.

But, no! Those words did not die -
Like a dormant volcano they did lie.

Within the deepest chamber of my heart
Since that day when we did part.
And today, when I saw you once more -
You beside your sweetheart, with happiness
galore,
That sleeping volcano deep within my heart
arose,
And those words came out, as a lava flows,
Not through my lips but through my eyes -
Tears of the love that never dies.

Sunshine Ahead

If life seems dull and painted grey,
And misfortune always blocks your way,
Mostly you encounter disappointments,
And if people hurt your sentiments -
Do not lose heart, and let down.
Remember sorrows will soon be gone.
Dark clouds will surely disappear,
So friends, dispel all your fears.
Keep the candle of hope burning bright,
That will give you the courage to fight
Against all disappointment and failure.
There's sunshine ahead, you can be sure.

Dream

Dream, O people! Dream, dream,
Dream of the life anew.
Dream, O people! Dream, dream,
Dream that your dreams come true.

Dream of what you long to be,
Dream of your heart's desire.
Dream of success, dream of joy,
Dream of soaring higher.

Dream of lending a helping hand,
Of standing by your friends,
Dream of sharing, caring,
Of setting selfless trends.

Dream of peace and harmony,
Of removing poverty,
Dream of a new and happy world,
Where there's global unity.

Dreams starting from ownself,
To the wide world around -
Only when you have a dream,
A direction can be found.

Dream, O people! Dream, dream -
That's nothing wrong at all,
And take it as the first step
Towards achieving your goal.

Once Again.....If

Give me back my childhood days,
Those joyful times, those playful ways.
When I had nothing to worry,
And when life to me was a fairy-story.
Ice-creams, chocolates, toys, and dolls,
Cycles, balloons, marbles, and balls,
Bedtime stories often told -
Such trifle joys made my world.
Learning felt like playful art,
Life began with a blissful start.
Gone are now those carefree times,
Those merry songs, and innocent rhymes.
Now, those sweet memories I cherish
And have just one ardent wish,
As I walk down memory lane -
To get back my childhood once again.

Spirit Of Life

The tender heart, hurt by the harsh world,
let out a deep sigh,
Dreary and lonely I sat through the night
gazing at the wide sky.
The darkness of the night gradually faded
ushering a new dawn,
The sky burst into a riot of colours with
the rising of the sun.
I turned my face towards the garden and
saw another crimson hue,
I wondered at the blooming rosebud—
soft petals kissed with dew.
The petals opened up slowly, shivering
in rapturous delight.
The meek crimson rose was glad to greet
the mighty crimson light.
Dancing butterflies teased the rose
and stole her nectar away.
Still she blushed merrily and seemed
ever-bright and gay.

A gentle breeze from its direction blew,
caressing my face and hair,
Soft whispers seemed to stir my soul
Thro the fragrance in the air.
"Give love and bring joy to every heart,
forget your own strife,
Share what you have and expect not—
That's the spirit of life."

Bring Peace To Our World

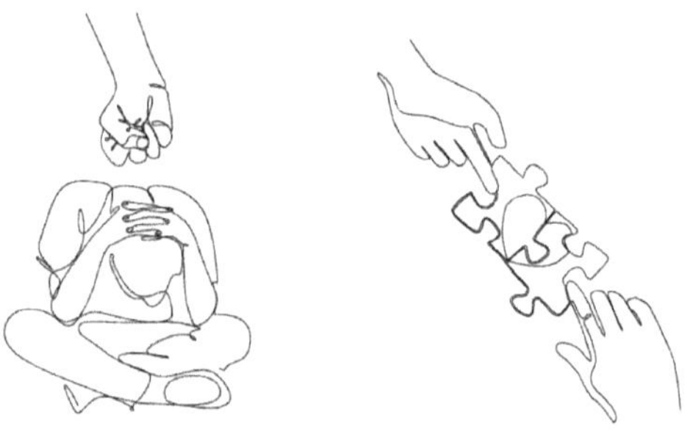

Each day we hear of endless bloodshed,
Of vengeance and of hatred.
Each of us struggles to dominate,
Seeking to acquire a superior state.
Our faces are etched with troubled looks,
We are always on tenterhooks.
We have lost our peace of mind,
We've forgotten to be good and kind.

God has given the quality
To each of us, of humanity.
Why can't we love one another?
And share all joys and sorrows together?
Banish from our mind all fears,
Try to brighten each face and wipe all tears.

The world would be a much better place
If only we could change our evil ways.

Face It

You are in control of each day,
You have the courage to carve your way.
You know that you have done no wrong,
So, you must stand steadfast and strong.
With a calm head and a resolute mind,
You can face turmoils of any kind.
Nobody knows what the future spells—
Today, you are in charge, nobody else.

Enchanted

In the stillness of the night,
When all around was calm and quiet,
As I lay awake in bed,
Sleepless eyes and a weary head,
I thought I heard a flute play,
From some place far, far away.
The flowing music stirred my soul,
And something within began to call,
To fall in tune with its rhythm.
Enchanted, as if in a dream,
I stepped out into open space,
As my bare feet touched the earth,
The warmth of the soft soil reached my heart.

A magnet pulled me out, I felt—
Into the field, where I knelt,
I bent down and kissed the ground,
And felt joyous music all around.
An unknown fragrance the earth let out,
Which enwrapped me all throughout.
I lay down as if in a spell,
And could hear Mother Earth softly tell -
Tales of far and near, new and old,
Tales which have never been told.
Like soft music, they fell on my ears.
By and by, the dark night clears -
Indeed, it was so enthralling!
Oh! such a divine, celestial feeling.

In Love With You

Sit beside me for a while,
Let me watch you as you smile,
Our eyes will speak our words of love
Together, our destiny we shall carve.

Let me hold your hands in mine
At this moment so serene, so divine,
Rest your head upon my shoulder,
Many a sweet thought let's wonder.

Under the moonlight, just you and me -
Let's vow—for each other, we shall be.
Two hearts beating to the same one tune,
Falling in love is indeed a boon.

The Pink Cloud

The desert land lay barren and dry,
Looking for its image up in the sky,
The sky gazed back at the arid land,
All that was seen were pebbles and sand.
Thus, the long, long days passed by,
The desert land looking at the wide wide sky.

Then, one day a soft pink cloud
Came floating by. The dry land felt so proud,
When the pink cloud smiled at her,
Stood there and gazed with wonder -
The pink cloud perhaps felt a bond,
With the desert - A lost love found.

The soft pink cloud showered from above,
And drenched the dry land with his love.
The dormant seeds that lay within
Sprouted, making the desert evergreen;
To the desert's life thus came spring,
Along with the love, which the cloud did
bring.

Me And My Candle

When I was in darkness -
My candle glowed bright
Pouring out its energy
So that I might find light.
The sighs it let out -
I never did hear,
Though in my solitude,
Only it was near.
Its tears that turned to vapour -
I never could see,
As the candle fought alone,
Burning only for me.
"Ungrateful" - I am not,
I know now its my turn -
Surely, a "THANKS" should suffice
As a prize in return.

So, I burnt out my candle,
Now I bask in daylight.
My selfless candle left no trace,
To remind me of the night.

Autumn's Symphony

The Earth is still fresh from bathing
In the monsoon's tender shower,
The fragrance of jasmine and tuberose
Still lingers in the bower.
Then, cool, pleasant breeze caress the trees,
Leaves and grasses kissed with dew -
As Autumn glides in stealthily,
To deck the earth anew.
Waves of kash flowers dress the fields
In a wavy, lacy gown,
While soft and light, white floating clouds
Form a veil upon its crown.
The careless beauty of shiuli flowers
Strewn all over the ground,
Earthy, musty smells broadcast
That Autumn is all around.

I Have Found New Hope

My near and dear ones, one by one,
Far from this madding crowd had gone
And I was left in the darkness all alone.
Deep within me, only a heavy moan,
My heart was heavy with unbearable sorrow,
I couldn't bear to face the morrow.

Then, I thought that I could hear
A faint murmuring from somewhere near.
Soon I realized what was it!
Yes, it was my own heart beat
Telling me, "You are not alone
The whole world is yours to call your own."

Now, I have a new urge to live,
My very best to the world to give.
No longer in the darkness do I grope.
For now, I have found new hope.
I want to lose myself among all,
And gladly depart when the Eternal shall call.

Humble Tribute To Mother Teresa

Without you, the world will never be the
same again,
You have left us in great sorrow and in pain.

You were the epitome of love and
compassion,
You were above all boundaries and all nation,
You were the apostle of peace and humanity,
You have always been the symbol of purity
You have shown the world how to love and
care
To you, O Mother, every life was dear.

O loving saint! You had risen above self,
To the sufferer you held out your hands to
help,
But there was not a hint of pride in you,
In your service, you were so noble and true.
Today, to the Eternal Abode you've gone to
rest,
After giving to this world your very best.

Mother Teresa! You are gone from the world today-
But the void created will forever stay.

Hope

A little thought I'd like to share -
Hold on to hope, even in despair.
If all lights fade out one by one,
Never let your hope be gone.
When luck fails you and dreams blow out
Only your hope can keep you afloat.
When you're laid down with sorrow,
Hope! Hope! Hope! for a better tomorrow.

Enchanting Fireflies

As the earth is draped in a soft dark veil,
Still of the night murmurs some strange,
faraway tale.
A wondrous sight of fairy lights dancing all
around,
Though there is no music playing nor there's
any sound.
Lights up my spirit, my mind soars high—
O! They are the fireflies - glowing as they fly!
The electric blue, the sparkling greens,
Like a floating shawl with shimmering
sequins.
Tiny drops of magic to brighten up the dark,
Even in the darkest hour - an enchanting
spark!

Through the night - dip, dip, dip! How the
fireflies dance-
But when sun comes and lifts the veil - all
seems like a trance.

Rhythm-without-rhythm

Life flows by in its own pace,
It follows no rhythm, time or space.
Time River washes away many a moment -
Life keeps no account of what's left, what's
spent.
Is age capable of understanding life's rhythm?
Years! They are bound by a rigid algorithm.
Every moment life poses a riddle -
The rhythm-lacking rhythm - we try to fiddle!
Still, I feel I might surely get a look
At the rhythms 'lucidated in life's book -
That day, I might paint on a new canvas.
To that rhythm-less rhythm, I shall dance!

Where years lose count of all the bygone
years,
Where silence speaks volumes without fears,
Where music can be heard without a tune -
There I shall I find life's true fortune!
One who flows with ones own intangible
wisdom,
Eccentricity of tune, beats and rhythm -
Someday I shall see through life's prism,
And triumph over that,
rhythm-without-rhythm.

A Butterfly's Rhapsody

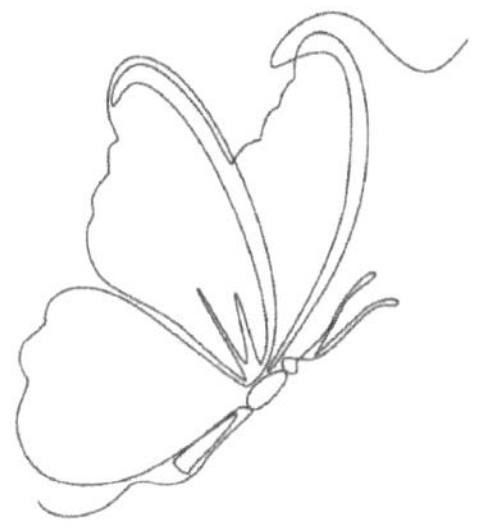

A butterfly flutters without a worry,
Weaving its small but sweet story,
Unfolding with each flap of its nimble dance,
The joyous spirit of a carefree essence.
On its chest, it carries no burden,
Though the next moment is uncertain.
Living in the moment, joy is what you
spread—
Love, life, and living! Not a moment to dread.
Flashing colours as you flap your wings about,
Your Rhapsody you perform without a doubt.

The Mother - The Tree

Born as a sapling, so tender and delicate,
Seeking water, seeking shadow, as was
appropriate,
She trembled under storms, and shivered in
the rain,
She learnt to take in her stride and endure all
pain.
As she grew, her roots spread wide and delved
deeper
Her trunk stood strong and she a vigil keeper.

A mother she becomes - caring for her
children naturally,
Love flows and spreads to each one
unconditionally.
The ones that cling on to her she provides
solace
With arms widespread she is ever-ready to
embrace,
When hurt by the harsh ones she bleeds her
sap,
But she doesn't bend nor does she snap—
Seeks support from her roots that nurtured
her with life's nectar
She continues her daily sonnet in life's altar.
Even when life ebbs away from her, yet she
does give
Her remains to serve so that the children may
live.